MEL BAY PRESENTS

THE *Fiddlin'* WORKSHOP

By Jeanine Orme

D1733044

CD CONTENTS

1	Soldier's Joy (including variations)	19	Ragtime Annie
2	Arkansas Traveler (including variation)	20	Crazy Creek
3	Devil's Dream (key of A)	21	Ook Pik
4	Devil's Dream (key of D)	22	Goodnight Waltz
5	Staten Island	23	Angus Campbell
6	Irish Washerwoman	24	Bill Cheatum
7	Garry Owen	25	Forester's Reel
8	Red Haired Boy	26	New Broom
9	Wilson's Clog	27	Snowflake Reel
10	Here's to the Ladies	28	Cuckoo's Nest (including variation)
11	St. Anne's Reel	29	Snowshoes
12	Great Western Clog	30	Forked Deer
13	East Tennessee Blues (twin fiddle)	31	Bittercreek
14	My Silver Bells (twin fiddle)	32	Salt River
15	Whoa Mule	33	Whiskey Before Breakfast
16	Fisher's Hornpipe	34	Cattle in the Cane
17	Teetotaler's Reel	35	Black & White Rag (including variation)
18	Temperance Reel	36	Little Joe

Fiddle-Jeanine Orme
Guitar-John Stewart, Bob Smesrud

1 2 3 4 5 6 7 8 9 0

TABLE OF CONTENTS

Introduction

This book was written to be used as a learning tool for beginners who have note reading ability. It presents very easy tunes to learn the basics of bowing and style, and progresses in difficulty with each tune. All of the arrangements are renditions that the author plays and has heard other fiddlers play. Many of the tunes are done in the style of Herman Johnson, a five-time National Fiddle Champion.

Each fiddle tune can be played in many different ways, and each fiddler has his or her own interpretation of how a song should be played. This book provides the tunes with usable fingerings, bowings and explanations.

Interpreting fiddle music by a book alone is very difficult. It is suggested that you also use the compact disc that is available with this book to hear the tunes played with accompaniment.

About the Author

Jeanine Rabe Orme was born in Ogden, Utah. She began playing the violin at age five, and began fiddling at age eight. During her youth, she performed with the Utah Old-time Fiddlers, and began entering fiddle contests. She has competed regularly at the Weiser National Old-time Fiddle Contest, as well as other national, state, and local contests. She is a past Utah State Champion and Oregon State Young Adult Champion.

Her music has been influenced significantly by Herman Johnson of Shawnee, Oklahoma. Mr. Johnson has instructed her in Texas-style fiddling, as well as swing.

Jeanine has been teaching fiddle lessons for over ten years. She has also played fiddle, bluegrass, and swing music with various bands in Utah and Oregon. Jeanine now resides in Beaverton, Oregon with her husband and two children.

Overview of Symbols and Terminology

Symbols

♪   slide up to the indicated note

♪   slide down from indicated note

⊓   down bow

V   up bow

♯   sharp-raises the pitch by a half step

♭   flat-lowers the pitch by a half step

♮   natural-pitch returns to its original state

♪   grace note-a grace note is part of the same beat as the note it precedes and is slurred quickly into the next note.

$^0_4$♪   The note is played with an open string and your 4th finger on the next lower string at the same time. For example, if the note was an A, you would play the open A string and with the 4th finger on the A note on the D string at the same time.

The section of music between the two repeat signs should be played twice.

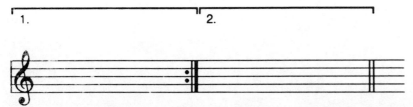

When you see a 1st and 2nd ending associated with repeating a section, play the 1st ending the first time and the 2nd ending the second time.

The notes connected with a slur should be played in the same bow stroke. A tie connects two notes with the same pitch and should also be played with the same bow stroke. When two notes of the same pitch are tied, the value of those two notes are combined.

Double Stop-Two notes are played at the same time.

Da capo (D.C.)-From the beginning

Fine-End

D.C. al Fine-This means to return to the beginning and play until you see the word "Fine."

Rhythm

Types of notes and rests

1 whole note=4 beats in 4/4 time

1 whole rest=4 beats of silence

2 half notes=1 whole note
A half note gets 2 beats

2 half rests=1 whole rest
A half rest gets 2 beats

4 quarter notes=1 whole note
A quarter note gets 1 beat

4 quarter rests=1 whole rest
A quarter rest gets 1 beat

8 eighth notes=1 whole note
An eighth note gets 1/2 of a beat

8 eighth rests=1 whole rest
An eighth rest gets 1/2 of a beat

16 sixteenth notes=1 whole note
A sixteenth note gets 1/4 of a beat

16 sixteenth rests=1 whole rest
A sixteenth rest gets 1/4 of a beat

Time Signature

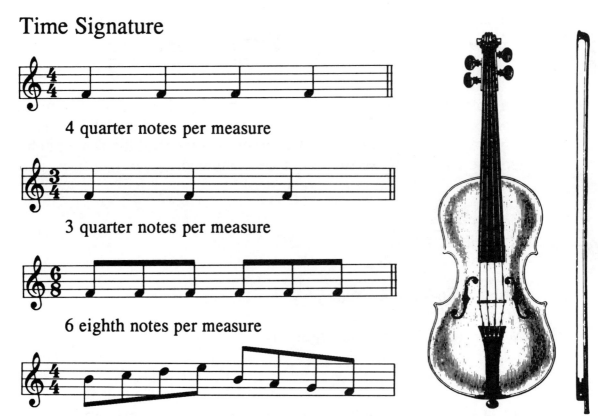

4 quarter notes per measure

3 quarter notes per measure

6 eighth notes per measure

Eighth notes and sixteenth notes are often connected by beams.

Triplet-Grouping of three notes played in the same time allotted to two notes of the same value. For example, an eighth note triplet ♫ would have the same value as two eighth notes ♫.

A dot after a note increases its time value by one half. For example, a dotted quarter note gets one and a half beats.

Swing Rhythm-The notation for a swing rhythm on a passage of eighth notes could be approximated as a dotted eighth note with a sixteenth note (or long-short, long-short)

The most important thing to learn in playing the fiddle is how to bow. You want to get a smooth (not choppy) sound. Using a swing rhythm on the indicated songs will help give a smooth flow, and the syncopation will change the mood and the whole sound of a song.

Scales and Key Signatures

The following key signatures are used in this book:

Major Key Signatures

Key of C   No sharps or flats

Key of G   One sharp - F#

Key of D   Two sharps - F# & C#

Key of A   Three sharps - F#, C# & G#

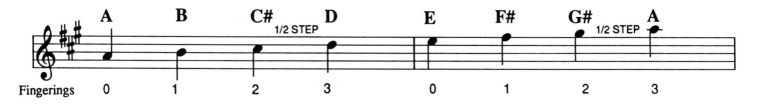

Fingerings are indicated underneath the scales. The half step markings show the fingers which should be placed close together as you play a song in this key.

SOLDIER'S JOY

Soldier's Joy is in the key of D with two sharps, F and C (see explanation of key signatures in Overview) Remember a slur means play both notes with the same bow stroke. (see also the explanation of repeat signs)

There are many ways to play most fiddle tunes. These are two variations for part B of Soldier's Joy.

ARKANSAS TRAVELER

Try w/ CD

Transitions

Arkansas Traveler is a reel with a familiar melody. Watch the rhythm in measure 2 (see explanation of dotted quarter in Overview).

Play root of Chords with CD

Par[...] [abo]ve lower as follows:

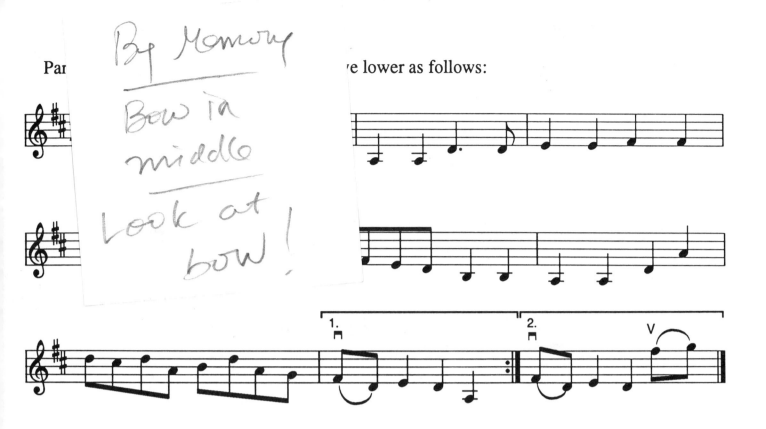

Handwritten note:
By Memory
Bow in middle
Look at bow!

DEVIL'S DREAM

Devil's Dream can be played in two different keys by simply starting on
different strings. It is traditionally played in the key of A with three sharps (see
explanation in Overview), but it has also been included in the key of D so that
it could be played in a medley with other D tunes. In measure three, the first
finger should be placed on both strings at the same time instead of moving the
finger from one string to the other.

DEVIL'S DREAM II

Traditional

STATEN ISLAND

In Staten Island you can use a more swingy rhythm on the eighth note passages (see explanation in Overview). This rhythm will give the song a different feel than playing straight eighth notes. In part **B** watch for the C♮ which is played with the second finger close to the first finger.

IRISH WASHERWOMAN

Irish Washerwoman is a traditional Irish jig. It is played in the key of G which has only one sharp. It is also in 6/8 time (see Overview).

Straight rhythm
Fast tempo

Traditional

GARRY OWEN

This is a traditional tune that could be played in a medley with "Irish Washerwoman." Slurs have been added for smoothness, but the song could be played without slurs.

"Garry Owen" is said to have been one of the songs played by a band as the 7th Cavalry headed out towards Little Big Horn. It was Custer's favorite battle tune.

Traditional

RED-HAIRED BOY

In old time fiddling each player has their own unique style, and you can hear different fiddlers play the same song with many variations. Improvisation is an important part of the development of different styles. "Red-Haired Boy" can be used as an example of how to change passages with simple improvisation. To give the tune a more swingy feel, use a swing rhythm on all eighth note passages.

Straight or swing rhythm
Moderate tempo

Traditional

Both versions could be played one after the other. This would add variety
and interest to the song if you are playing it through more than once.

(Variation)

WILSON'S CLOG

"Wilson's Clog" is also known as "Fred Wilson's Clog" or "Fred Wilson's Hornpipe." It is written here in 6/8 time to make the rhythm easier to read.

Traditional

Fast or Moderate tempo

HERE'S TO THE LADIES

Also known as "To the Ladies." The use of triplets and double stops is introduced in this tune. (See Overview)

Straight rhythm
Fast tempo

Traditional

ST. ANNE'S REEL

Again this version uses triplets and double stops which give an Irish feel.
The notes in the double stops are both fingered, so it is very important to
have both notes precisely in tune.

Swing rhythm
Fast or moderate tempo

Traditional

GREAT WESTERN CLOG

This clog is also known as the "Great Western Lancashire Clog." It has been written in 6/8 time to make the rhythm easier to read. This song probably originated in the British Isles and would be most popular among Canadian style fiddlers.

Moderate tempo

Traditional

EAST TENNESSEE BLUES

"East Tennessee Blues" is a popular fiddle tune which works very well with two fiddles in harmony. Use a swing rhythm pattern.

Swing rhythm
Fast or moderate tempo

Old-time

*This version is based on the playing of Bobby Hicks (see discography).

MY SILVER BELLS

This is another popular fiddle tune arranged for two fiddles. Use a swing rhythm pattern.

Swing rhythm
Fast or moderate tempo

Old-time

*This version is based on the playing of Ricky Boen and Wes Westmoreland III.

WHOA MULE

Whoa Mule uses finger slides to imitate the sound of a mule. The symbol /
means to slide your finger up to the note.

Swing rhythm
Fast or moderate tempo

Traditional

FISHER'S HORNPIPE

Fisher's hornpipe is a popular tune that is played often in fiddle contests. This version is in the key of D, but it is common to hear it played in the key of F. Three note slurs have been added to make a smooth flow of notes.

THE TEETOTALLER'S REEL

The Teetotaller's Reel and Temperance Reel are two different versions of the same tune which is also known as Kingsport or The Devil in Georgia. The two different versions can represent the contrast in styles of fiddling. The Teetotaller's Reel is done in a very traditional old time style.

Straight rhythm
Fast or moderate tempo

Traditional

TEMPERANCE REEL

Temperance Reel has some added improvisation to give a different sound. Be sure to swing the rhythm. In the first measure of section B, the E note should be played on the open E string and with the 4th finger on the E note on the A string.

RAGTIME ANNIE

This is a very popular old time fiddle tune. This variation starts by sliding from an F♮ into an F♯. After the slide, leave the second finger on the string throughout the first three measures. The double stops give this tune a very old timey sound.

STRAIGHT RHYTHM
FAST OR MODERATE
TEMPO

Traditional

CRAZY CREEK

Crazy Creek, which has a very unique sound, is best known as a bluegrass instrumental. (See overview for explanation of D.C. al fine)

Swing rhythm
Fast or moderate tempo

Traditional

WALTZES

A fiddle waltz is any danceable waltz played in a fiddle style. The following waltzes are common waltzes played in a fiddle contests. They should be played with very smooth long bow strokes. The symbol / means to slide the finger up to the note. Sliding into notes and using double stops are common techniques in playing fiddle style waltzes.

OOK PIK

Swing rhythm on eighth notes
Danceable waltz tempo

GOODNIGHT WALTZ

The guitar chords marked in parentheses are optional chords which can be added for more variety.

Swing rhythm on eighth notes
Danceable waltz tempo

TEXAS STYLE FIDDLING

Texas style fiddling is a distinct style that brings elements of swing and jazz into the traditional oldtime fiddle tunes. A player improvises passages of the tune to add variety. Players also listen to each other and mimic each other's playing. The style began in Texas with players such as Major Franklin, Lewis Franklin, Vernon Solomon and Benny Thomason. Benny Thomason helped introduce the style to contests like the Weiser National Oldtime Fiddle Contest, and he has taught many young fiddlers such as Mark O'Connor.

The following tunes are often played among Texas style fiddlers and in fiddle contests. The versions are basic and have workable bowings. The tunes will serve as a good start in learning Texas style fiddling.

ANGUS CAMPBELL

Swing Rhythm
Fast or moderate tempo

Traditional

In the style of Herman Johnson

BILL CHEATUM

Swing Rhythm
Fast or moderate tempo

Traditional

In the style of Herman Johnson

FORESTER'S REEL

Swing Rhythm
Fast or moderate tempo

Traditional

In the style of Herman Johnson

NEW BROOM

Swing Rhythm
Fast or moderate tempo

Traditional

In the style of Herman Johnson

SNOWFLAKE REEL

Swing Rhythm
Fast tempo

Traditional

In the style of Herman Johnson

CUCKOO'S NEST

Two versions of the Cuckoo's Nest are given here to show a contrast in styles. The first is a very traditional version.

Traditional

Swing rhythm
Moderate tempo

This version of Cuckoo's nest shows how improvisation can be used to add variety to a simple melody. In part A, measures 1 and 3 you can try your own improvisation by adding notes between the quarter notes.

In the style of Benny Thomason

SNOWSHOES

Swing Rhythm
Fast or moderate tempo

Traditional

In the style of Herman Johnson

FORKED DEER

Traditional

Swing rhythm
Moderate tempo

An open A string can be added as a double stop to the last measure of part A and double stops can be added to the last three measures of part B as follows.

BITTERCREEK

Swing rhythm
Fast or moderate tempo

TRADITIONAL

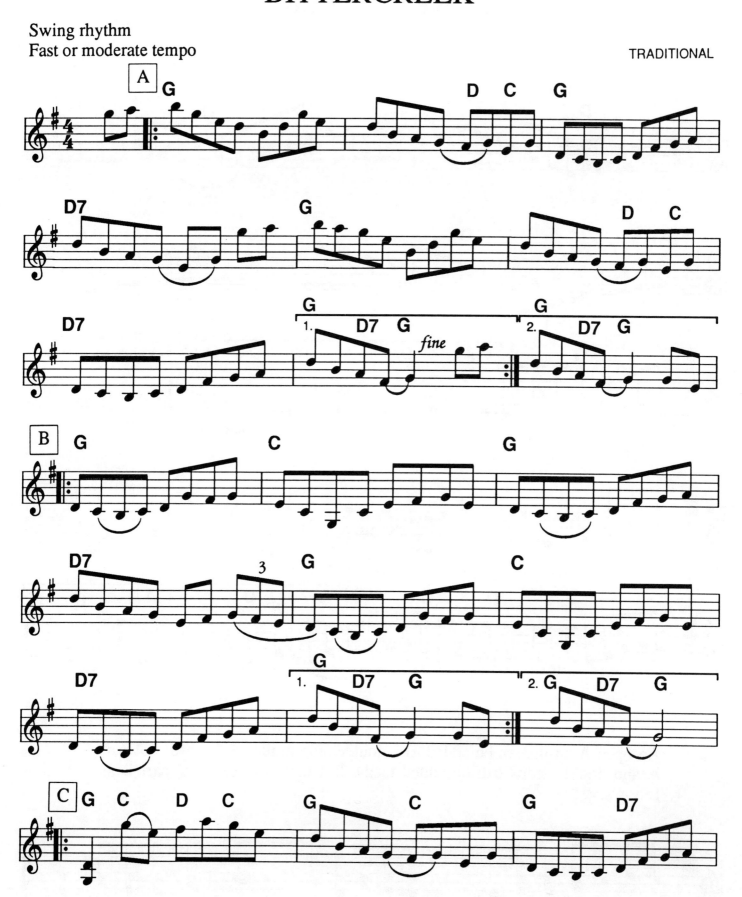

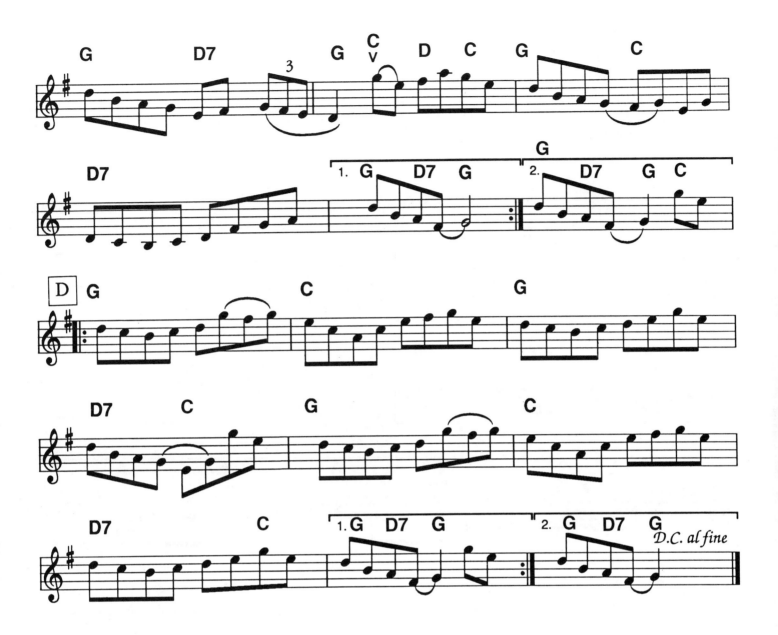

In the style of Herman Johnson

53

SALT RIVER

This tune is as popular among bluegrass musicians as Salt Creek. In a bluegrass setting it should be played at a fast tempo and a straight rhythm. Played as a Texas style hoedown, Salt River should have more of a swing rhythm and a moderate tempo.

Traditional

In the style of Herman Johnson

WHISKEY BEFORE BREAKFAST

Swing rhythm
Fast or moderate tempo

Traditional

CATTLE IN THE CANE

Swing rhythm
Fast or moderate tempo

In the style of Herman Johnson

Traditionally the A and B parts of this song would be switched in order.

BLACK & WHITE RAG

Swing rhythm
Fast or moderate tempo

George Botsford

Variation: B

In the style of Herman Johnson

LITTLE JOE

Swing rhythm
Moderate tempo

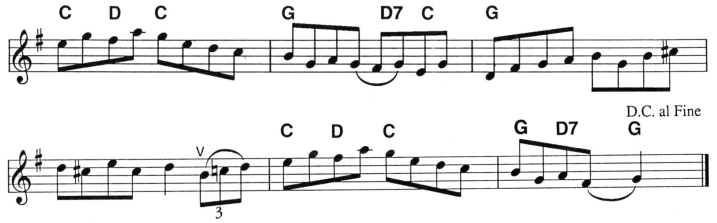

In the style of Herman Johnson

ABOUT FIDDLE CONTESTS

For those who play the fiddle, but have never played in a fiddle contest, this information will help answer questions about how contests work.

In most contests, like the Weiser National Oldtime Fiddle Contest, the contestant must play a hoedown, a waltz, and a tune of choice in each round.

A hoedown is difficult to define, but any tune which is called a breakdown, hornpipe, or reel would be considered a hoedown. It should be played in 2/4 or 4/4 time signature, and is generally played faster than the tune of choice.

The fiddle waltz is any danceable waltz played in a fiddle style. A fiddle style waltz can have vibrato, but fiddlers usually use a very slow vibrato as opposed to a fast classical vibrato.

A tune other than a hoedown or waltz would be a tune of choice. Any rag, polka, jig, or song played in 6/8 time is appropriate if it is played at a danceable tempo. Some general rules apply to all tunes. There is no cross tuning allowed on stage, and you cannot use any "trick or fancy fiddling" such as shuffle bowing. This eliminates songs like "Orange Blossom Special", "Black Mountain Rag", and other show tunes.

Most contests score each tune with points allotted to categories such as rhythm, tone quality, oldtime fiddling ability and danceability.

Contests vary wherever you go. It is a good idea to get familiar with the rules of a contest before you play in it. If you have any questions, ask the judges or other fiddlers. Always listen and try to learn tunes from the other fiddle players.

DISCOGRAPHY

The best place to find fiddle albums is at fiddle contests where many fiddle champions have albums for sale. Some fiddle albums can be found in record shops and through mail order catalogues. I have taken ideas for the songs in this book from the following albums:

1. American Heritage 1-Championship Fiddling (Herman Johnson) P-120-1
2. John's-National Champion (Herman Johnson) 677805
3. Texas Crapshooter (Bobby Hicks) County 772
4. Westex Records-In The Mood (Wes Westmoreland and Ricky Boen) WR1581
5. John's-Benny Thomason, Volume Two BT-48015
6. John Francis-Fiddler Album No. 2
7. Rounder 137-Soppin' The Gravy (Mark O'Connor) R-0137